The United States

Louisiana

Anne Welsbacher

ABDO & Daughters

visit us at
www.abdopub.com

Published by Abdo & Daughters, 4940 Viking Drive, Suite 622, Edina, Minnesota 55435.

Printed in the United States.

Cover and Interior Photo credits: Archive Photos, Peter Arnold, Inc., Super Stock

Edited by Lori Kinstad Pupeza
Contributing editor Brooke Henderson
Special thanks to our Checkerboard Kids—Francesca Tuminelly, Raymond Sherman, Laura Jones

All statistics taken from the 1990 census; The Rand McNally Discovery Atlas of The United States. Other sources: *Louisiana*, Fradin and Fradin, Children's Press, Chicago, 1995; *Louisiana*, Kent, Children's Press, Chicago, 1988; *Louisiana*, LaDoux, Lerner Publications Co., Minneapolis, 1993; America Online, Compton's Living Encyclopedia, 1997; World Book Encyclopedia, 1990.

Library of Congress Cataloging-in-Publication Data

Welsbacher, Anne, 1955-
Louisiana / Anne Welsbacher.
p. cm. -- (United States)
Includes index.
Summary: Presents information about the history, geography, people, recreation, and economy of the state of Louisisana.
ISBN 1-56239-880-6
1. Louisiana--Juvenile literature. 2. Louisiana. I. Title. II. Series: United States (Series)
F369.3.W45 1998
976.3--dc21
97-24614
CIP
AC

Contents

Welcome to Louisiana

The mighty Mississippi River runs all the way through the United States. It begins in the north, near Canada. It ends in Louisiana at the **Gulf** of Mexico.

French, African American, Native American, and Spanish people came together in Louisiana. They mixed their religion, music, food, and clothes.

Louisiana people made new music and new food. They spoke new languages. They started a world-famous **festival**. They even made a new kind of sugar!

Opposite page: The swamps of Louisiana.

Fast Facts

LOUISIANA

Capital
Baton Rouge (219,531 people)
Area
44,520 square miles
(115,306 sq km)
Population
4,238,216 people
Rank: 21st
Statehood
April 30, 1812
(18th state admitted)
Principal rivers
Mississippi River
Red River
Sabine River
Highest point
Driskill Mountain;
535 feet (163 m)
Largest City
New Orleans (496,938 People)
Motto
Union, justice, and confidence
Song
"Give Me Louisiana"
Famous People
Louis Armstrong, Pierre Beauregard, Lillian Hellman, Huey Long, Mahalia Jackson

State Flag

Magnolia

Brown Pelican

Bald Cypress

About Louisiana

The Pelican State

Borders: west (Texas), north (Arkansas), east (Mississippi), south (Gulf of Mexico)

Nature's Treasures

The river brings many treasures into Louisiana's soil. It brings peat, clay, and good farming soil. The dirt that a river carries onto the land is called **silt**.

Louisiana's land holds much gas and oil. It also has salt and sulfur.

Louisiana has many forms of water. The **Gulf** Coast of the ocean forms swamps and **bayous**. Bayous are formed by rivers and ocean waters joining.

The **delta** from the Mississippi is very big. If you made four copies of the Mississippi Delta, they would fill all of Louisiana!

Louisiana sometimes has hurricanes. Hurricanes are huge storms that are formed over oceans. They can knock down buildings. They can hurt or kill people.

Louisiana is **humid**. Louisiana is one of the wettest states in the country.

An oil drilling platform in the Mississippi Delta, Louisiana.

Beginnings

The first Louisianians were Native Americans who lived 12,000 years ago! By the 1600s, there were the Caddo, Chitimacha, Natchez, Tunica, and other groups of Native Americans. Many lived along the Mississippi River in houses built on stilts.

In 1682, a French explorer claimed the area for his country. He named it Louisiana, after the French **King Louis XIV**.

In the 1700s, French settlers came. Other settlers came from Spain and Canada. The settlers brought slaves from Africa to farm the land. They forced many Native Americans out of the area.

In 1803, the French sold Louisiana and other states to the new United States. In 1812, Louisiana became the 18th state.

The South wanted slavery but the North did not. Louisiana and other southern states **seceded** from the United States.

In 1861, the South and the North fought the Civil War over slavery. The North won the war in 1865. Much in the South was gone. Louisiana lost more people and buildings than most of the other southern states.

In the 1870s and 1880s, the North tried to help the South rebuild. This was called the **Reconstruction** period. Then the North stopped helping the South.

African Americans still did not have as many rights as white people in southern states. In some schools, all the students were white. In other schools, all the students were African American. People were **segregated**, or kept apart.

In the 1950s and 1960s, the Civil Rights movement was born. People fought for **integration** and other rights.

In 1960, a court ordered an all-white public school to start allowing African-American students to attend. This was the first time there was integration in Louisiana.

B.C. through 1700s

The First Louisianians

10,000 B.C.: About 30 different groups of Native Americans live in Louisiana area. The largest group are the Caddo.

1682: A French explorer claims Louisiana for France.

Through 1700s: Settlers from Europe force almost all Native Americans out of the area. Most are gone by 1859.

Louisiana

B.C. through 1700s

1795 to 1812

Rolling down the River

1795: A new way is found to make sugar from the sugarcane plant.

1803: France sells its land in Louisiana to the United States.

1812: Louisiana becomes a state.

1812: The first steamboat rolls down the Mississippi River to Louisiana.

Louisiana

1795 to 1812

1838 to Today

Into Today

1838: The first **Mardi Gras** parade is held.

1861: Louisiana **secedes** from the United States. The Civil War begins.

1901: The first oil well in Louisiana is drilled.

1927: Dixieland Jazz becomes popular.

1975: The world's largest indoor stadium opens in New Orleans.

Louisiana

1838 to Today

Louisiana's People

There are more than four million people in Louisiana. Many live in cities. Others live in the country.

Many of the people who came to Louisiana from France, Spain, the West Indies, and Africa married each other. They had children. Those children had children! They were called **Creoles**.

Some people came from Canada. They spoke a new kind of language. It was a mix of French and other languages. They were called **Cajun**.

Today, there are still Creoles and Cajuns in Louisiana. Many Louisianians are African American. Many others are white. A few are Italian American and Vietnamese American.

Jazz trumpet player Louis Armstrong and trumpet player Wynton Marsalis were both born in New Orleans,

Louisiana. Rock and roll singer Jerry Lee Lewis was born in Ferriday, Louisiana. Piano player Van Cliburn was born in Shreveport, Louisiana.

Truman Capote was born in New Orleans. He was a famous writer. Many of his stories were about when he was a little boy.

Gospel singer Mahalia Jackson was from New Orleans. Anne Rice is from New Orleans. She writes stories about vampires!

Jerry Lee Lewis

Louis Armstrong

Louisiana's Cities

New Orleans is the biggest city in Louisiana. Many people from around the world visit New Orleans. It has many places to eat and listen to music. A well-known area in New Orleans is called the French Quarter.

The capital is Baton Rouge. It is a Mississippi **port** city. Boats come and go from Baton Rouge.

Shreveport is home of the state fair. Other towns in Louisiana are Lafayette and Lake Charles.

Opposite page: Bourbon St., the French Quarter in New Orleans, Louisiana.

Seaport
CAFE & BAR
Memories
Temptation
T-SHIRTS·GIFTS

Louisiana's Land

The South has 13 states. Louisiana is in the **Deep South**. That means it is one of the most southern states.

Louisiana is shaped like a boot. The boot points to the east. At the toe is New Orleans. The bottom of the boot walks along the ocean!

Water that is next to land is called a **gulf**. South of Louisiana is the Gulf of Mexico. Texas is west of Louisiana. Arkansas is north. Mississippi is east. Louisiana has many **marshes** and salt domes.

Much of Louisiana has forests. Magnolias, pines, oak, and cypress trees grow in the forests. Spanish moss hangs from some of the trees! Honeysuckle, **azaleas**, lilies, and jasmine are some Louisiana flowers.

Opposite page: Cypress Swamp, Louisiana.

Alligators live in the swamps of Louisiana. Rays and shrimp swim in the ocean waters on Louisiana's coast. Rabbits and gray foxes run through the hills. Wild hogs, raccoons, and skunks are other animals in Louisiana.

The brown pelican is Louisiana's state bird. Other birds in Louisiana are egrets, quails, doves, and wild turkeys.

Louisiana at Play

Many people all over the country love to play in New Orleans, Louisiana! A special music called **jazz** was born in New Orleans. The city also is world famous for its food.

Every spring, people dress up and parade through the streets. They act silly, dance, and eat lots of good food. The parade is called **Mardi Gras**.

The New Year's Day Sugar Bowl is played in New Orleans. The city also has a big **aquarium** next to the ocean. An aquarium is like a zoo for fish!

Avery Island is in the **marshes** of Louisiana. People see many plants and birds in the Avery Island Jungle Gardens.

Louisiana has many parks. Some of them show what the Civil War battles were like. Others have areas for camping, fishing, and swimming.

Louisianians love food. And they love **festivals**! A festival is like a big party outside.

In any year in Louisiana, you can go to a tomato festival, a crab festival, a French food festival, or a rice festival! You can even go to a frog festival!

Mardi Gras in New Orleans, Louisiana.

Louisiana at Work

Louisiana has a large service **industry**. That means people from other places visit Louisiana. Louisianians work to serve them. For example, they cook and serve food.

Many people mine gas and oil. Louisiana has more mining than any state except Texas.

There is a lot of fishing in Louisiana. More shrimp is fished in Louisiana than any other state. People also catch oysters and blue crabs.

Moving things around is another kind of job in Louisiana! Ships come in from the ocean. Cars and trains cross its bridges. And boats still float down the mighty Mississippi River!

Opposite page: Shrimp boats.

MURDOCK
MURDOCK
MONA LISA
MONA LISA
JET STREAM

Fun Facts

•The longest boxing match in history was in Louisiana. It lasted for over seven hours!
•A very hot tasting sauce is made in Louisiana. It is called Tabasco sauce. It was first made in 1868.
•Almost all the crayfish made for eating in the world are from Louisiana.
•The oldest cathedral in America, the St. Louis Cathedral, is in Louisiana. It was built in 1716.
•Louisiana has had opera shows since the early 1800s. The shows are often in English, Italian, and French.
•The world's longest bridge is over Lake Pontchartrain, near New Orleans, Louisiana. It is 24 miles long!

The St. Louis Cathedral in Louisiana.

Glossary

Aquarium: a glass box that holds fish and other sea creatures. Like a zoo for marine life.
Azalea: a kind of bush with flowers.
Bayou: a body of water like a lake. It is formed by rivers and ocean waters joining.
Cajun: a person born of people from French-speaking Canada. Cajun is also a kind of cooking. It is usually very spicy! Cajun is special to Louisiana.
Creole: a person born of people from France and Africa or other countries. Creole is special to Louisiana.
Deep South: the states in the farthest part of the United States called the South.
Delta: a stretch of land made by the silt from a river.
Festival: a big party, usually for a whole city. A festival often has a parade, music, and food.
Gulf: water that is next to land.
Humid: air that is very wet, and feels moist and sticky.
Industry: any kind of business.
Integrate: to mix together, opposite of segregate.
Jazz: an American kind of music that first was played in Louisiana.
King Louis XIV: the king of France in the 1600s. Louisiana was named for him.
Mardi Gras: a special festival that happens every spring in New Orleans.
Marsh: very wet land, like a swamp.
Port: a place next to the water, where boats can park.
Reconstruction: a time in U.S. history following the Civil War. The North helped the South rebuild their houses, land, and jobs. But then they quit helping. The South was still very poor.

Secede: to break away, to leave the Union.
Segregate: to keep separate and apart, opposite of integrate.
Silt: dirt that a river carries onto the land.
Wetland: land that has much water in it, and feels spongy.

Internet Sites

The Gumbo Pages
http://www.gumbopages.com
Hey, where y'at! Welcome to The Gumbo Pages, a musical, culinary, and cultural information source about New Orleans and Acadiana (or "Cajun country"). I've also got lots of nifty stuff about roots music, noncommercial radio, and just about anything else that interests me.

Mardi G. Raccoon–Louisiana's Ambassador of Fun
http://www.mardi.com
Hi, I'm Mardi G. Raccoon. I live in City Park, in New Orleans. Here on my new web site, you will find cool places and things for Kids in New Orleans, and other parts of Louisiana.

These sites are subject to change. Go to your favorite search engine and type in Louisiana for more sites.

PASS IT ON

Tell Others Something Special About Your State

To educate readers around the country, pass on interesting tips, places to see, history, and little unknown facts about the state you live in. We want to hear from you!

To get posted on ABDO & Daughters website E-mail us at "mystate@abdopub.com"

Index